My First Password Keeper

This Book belongs to

_____

_____

_____

_____

WEBSITE NAME

USERNAME

PASSWORD

EMAIL

NOTE

WEBSITE NAME

USERNAME

PASSWORD

EMAIL

NOTE

WEBSITE NAME

USERNAME

PASSWORD

EMAIL

NOTE

WEBSITE NAME

USERNAME

PASSWORD

EMAIL

NOTE

WEBSITE NAME

USERNAME

PASSWORD

EMAIL

NOTE

WEBSITE NAME

USERNAME

PASSWORD

EMAIL

NOTE

WEBSITE NAME

USERNAME

PASSWORD

EMAIL

NOTE

WEBSITE NAME

USERNAME

PASSWORD

EMAIL

NOTE

WEBSITE NAME

USERNAME

PASSWORD

EMAIL

NOTE

WEBSITE NAME

USERNAME

PASSWORD

EMAIL

NOTE

WEBSITE NAME

USERNAME

PASSWORD

EMAIL

NOTE

WEBSITE NAME

USERNAME

PASSWORD

EMAIL

NOTE

WEBSITE NAME

USERNAME

PASSWORD

EMAIL

NOTE

WEBSITE NAME

USERNAME

PASSWORD

EMAIL

NOTE

WEBSITE NAME

USERNAME

PASSWORD

EMAIL

NOTE

WEBSITE NAME

USERNAME

PASSWORD

EMAIL

NOTE

WEBSITE NAME

USERNAME

PASSWORD

EMAIL

NOTE

WEBSITE NAME

USERNAME

PASSWORD

EMAIL

NOTE

WEBSITE NAME

USERNAME

PASSWORD

EMAIL

NOTE

WEBSITE NAME

USERNAME

PASSWORD

EMAIL

NOTE

WEBSITE NAME

USERNAME

PASSWORD

EMAIL

NOTE

WEBSITE NAME

USERNAME

PASSWORD

EMAIL

NOTE

WEBSITE NAME

USERNAME

PASSWORD

EMAIL

NOTE

WEBSITE NAME

USERNAME

PASSWORD

EMAIL

NOTE

WEBSITE NAME

USERNAME

PASSWORD

EMAIL

NOTE

WEBSITE NAME

USERNAME

PASSWORD

EMAIL

NOTE

WEBSITE NAME

USERNAME

PASSWORD

EMAIL

NOTE

WEBSITE NAME

USERNAME

PASSWORD

EMAIL

NOTE

WEBSITE NAME

USERNAME

PASSWORD

EMAIL

NOTE

WEBSITE NAME

USERNAME

PASSWORD

EMAIL

NOTE

WEBSITE NAME

USERNAME

PASSWORD

EMAIL

NOTE

WEBSITE NAME

USERNAME

PASSWORD

EMAIL

NOTE

WEBSITE NAME

USERNAME

PASSWORD

EMAIL

NOTE

WEBSITE NAME

USERNAME

PASSWORD

EMAIL

NOTE

WEBSITE NAME

USERNAME

PASSWORD

EMAIL

NOTE

WEBSITE NAME

USERNAME

PASSWORD

EMAIL

NOTE

WEBSITE NAME

USERNAME

PASSWORD

EMAIL

NOTE

WEBSITE NAME

USERNAME

PASSWORD

EMAIL

NOTE

WEBSITE NAME

USERNAME

PASSWORD

EMAIL

NOTE

WEBSITE NAME

USERNAME

PASSWORD

EMAIL

NOTE

WEBSITE NAME

USERNAME

PASSWORD

EMAIL

NOTE

WEBSITE NAME

USERNAME

PASSWORD

EMAIL

NOTE

WEBSITE NAME

USERNAME

PASSWORD

EMAIL

NOTE

WEBSITE NAME

USERNAME

PASSWORD

EMAIL

NOTE

WEBSITE NAME

USERNAME
_____

PASSWORD
_____

EMAIL
_____

NOTE
_____

WEBSITE NAME

USERNAME
_____

PASSWORD
_____

EMAIL
_____

NOTE
_____

WEBSITE NAME

USERNAME
_____

PASSWORD
_____

EMAIL
_____

NOTE
_____

WEBSITE NAME

USERNAME
_____

PASSWORD
_____

EMAIL
_____

NOTE
_____

WEBSITE NAME

USERNAME

PASSWORD

EMAIL

NOTE

WEBSITE NAME

USERNAME

PASSWORD

EMAIL

NOTE

WEBSITE NAME

USERNAME

PASSWORD

EMAIL

NOTE

WEBSITE NAME

USERNAME

PASSWORD

EMAIL

NOTE

WEBSITE NAME

USERNAME

PASSWORD

EMAIL

NOTE

WEBSITE NAME

USERNAME

PASSWORD

EMAIL

NOTE

WEBSITE NAME

USERNAME

PASSWORD

EMAIL

NOTE

WEBSITE NAME

USERNAME

PASSWORD

EMAIL

NOTE

WEBSITE NAME

USERNAME

PASSWORD

EMAIL

NOTE

WEBSITE NAME

USERNAME

PASSWORD

EMAIL

NOTE

WEBSITE NAME

USERNAME

PASSWORD

EMAIL

NOTE

WEBSITE NAME

USERNAME

PASSWORD

EMAIL

NOTE

WEBSITE NAME

USERNAME

PASSWORD

EMAIL

NOTE

WEBSITE NAME

USERNAME

PASSWORD

EMAIL

NOTE

WEBSITE NAME

USERNAME

PASSWORD

EMAIL

NOTE

WEBSITE NAME

USERNAME

PASSWORD

EMAIL

NOTE

WEBSITE NAME

USERNAME

PASSWORD

EMAIL

NOTE

WEBSITE NAME

USERNAME

PASSWORD

EMAIL

NOTE

WEBSITE NAME

USERNAME

PASSWORD

EMAIL

NOTE

WEBSITE NAME

USERNAME

PASSWORD

EMAIL

NOTE

WEBSITE NAME

USERNAME

PASSWORD

EMAIL

NOTE

WEBSITE NAME

USERNAME

PASSWORD

EMAIL

NOTE

WEBSITE NAME

USERNAME

PASSWORD

EMAIL

NOTE

WEBSITE NAME

USERNAME

PASSWORD

EMAIL

NOTE

WEBSITE NAME

USERNAME

PASSWORD

EMAIL

NOTE

WEBSITE NAME

USERNAME

PASSWORD

EMAIL

NOTE

WEBSITE NAME

USERNAME

PASSWORD

EMAIL

NOTE

WEBSITE NAME

USERNAME

PASSWORD

EMAIL

NOTE

WEBSITE NAME

USERNAME

PASSWORD

EMAIL

NOTE

WEBSITE NAME

USERNAME

PASSWORD

EMAIL

NOTE

WEBSITE NAME

USERNAME

PASSWORD

EMAIL

NOTE

WEBSITE NAME

USERNAME

PASSWORD

EMAIL

NOTE

WEBSITE NAME

USERNAME

PASSWORD

EMAIL

NOTE

WEBSITE NAME

USERNAME

PASSWORD

EMAIL

NOTE

WEBSITE NAME

USERNAME

PASSWORD

EMAIL

NOTE

WEBSITE NAME

USERNAME

PASSWORD

EMAIL

NOTE

WEBSITE NAME

USERNAME

PASSWORD

EMAIL

NOTE

WEBSITE NAME

USERNAME

PASSWORD

EMAIL

NOTE

WEBSITE NAME

USERNAME

PASSWORD

EMAIL

NOTE

WEBSITE NAME

USERNAME

PASSWORD

EMAIL

NOTE

WEBSITE NAME

USERNAME

PASSWORD

EMAIL

NOTE

WEBSITE NAME

USERNAME

PASSWORD

EMAIL

NOTE

WEBSITE NAME

USERNAME

PASSWORD

EMAIL

NOTE

WEBSITE NAME

USERNAME

PASSWORD

EMAIL

NOTE

WEBSITE NAME

USERNAME

PASSWORD

EMAIL

NOTE

WEBSITE NAME

USERNAME

PASSWORD

EMAIL

NOTE

WEBSITE NAME

USERNAME

PASSWORD

EMAIL

NOTE

WEBSITE NAME

USERNAME

PASSWORD

EMAIL

NOTE

WEBSITE NAME

USERNAME
_____

PASSWORD
_____

EMAIL
_____

NOTE
_____

WEBSITE NAME

USERNAME
_____

PASSWORD
_____

EMAIL
_____

NOTE
_____

WEBSITE NAME

USERNAME
_____

PASSWORD
_____

EMAIL
_____

NOTE
_____

WEBSITE NAME

USERNAME
_____

PASSWORD
_____

EMAIL
_____

NOTE
_____

WEBSITE NAME

USERNAME

PASSWORD

EMAIL

NOTE

WEBSITE NAME

USERNAME

PASSWORD

EMAIL

NOTE

WEBSITE NAME

USERNAME

PASSWORD

EMAIL

NOTE

WEBSITE NAME

USERNAME

PASSWORD

EMAIL

NOTE

WEBSITE NAME

USERNAME

PASSWORD

EMAIL

NOTE

WEBSITE NAME

USERNAME

PASSWORD

EMAIL

NOTE

WEBSITE NAME

USERNAME

PASSWORD

EMAIL

NOTE

WEBSITE NAME

USERNAME

PASSWORD

EMAIL

NOTE

WEBSITE NAME

USERNAME

PASSWORD

EMAIL

NOTE

WEBSITE NAME

USERNAME

PASSWORD

EMAIL

NOTE

WEBSITE NAME

USERNAME

PASSWORD

EMAIL

NOTE

WEBSITE NAME

USERNAME

PASSWORD

EMAIL

NOTE

WEBSITE NAME

USERNAME

PASSWORD

EMAIL

NOTE

WEBSITE NAME

USERNAME

PASSWORD

EMAIL

NOTE

WEBSITE NAME

USERNAME

PASSWORD

EMAIL

NOTE

WEBSITE NAME

USERNAME

PASSWORD

EMAIL

NOTE

WEBSITE NAME

USERNAME
_____

PASSWORD
_____

EMAIL
_____

NOTE
_____

WEBSITE NAME

USERNAME
_____

PASSWORD
_____

EMAIL
_____

NOTE
_____

WEBSITE NAME

USERNAME
_____

PASSWORD
_____

EMAIL
_____

NOTE
_____

WEBSITE NAME

USERNAME
_____

PASSWORD
_____

EMAIL
_____

NOTE
_____

WEBSITE NAME

USERNAME

PASSWORD

EMAIL

NOTE

WEBSITE NAME

USERNAME

PASSWORD

EMAIL

NOTE

WEBSITE NAME

USERNAME

PASSWORD

EMAIL

NOTE

WEBSITE NAME

USERNAME

PASSWORD

EMAIL

NOTE

WEBSITE NAME

USERNAME

PASSWORD

EMAIL

NOTE

WEBSITE NAME

USERNAME

PASSWORD

EMAIL

NOTE

WEBSITE NAME

USERNAME

PASSWORD

EMAIL

NOTE

WEBSITE NAME

USERNAME

PASSWORD

EMAIL

NOTE

WEBSITE NAME

USERNAME

PASSWORD

EMAIL

NOTE

WEBSITE NAME

USERNAME

PASSWORD

EMAIL

NOTE

WEBSITE NAME

USERNAME

PASSWORD

EMAIL

NOTE

WEBSITE NAME

USERNAME

PASSWORD

EMAIL

NOTE

WEBSITE NAME

USERNAME

PASSWORD

EMAIL

NOTE

WEBSITE NAME

USERNAME

PASSWORD

EMAIL

NOTE

WEBSITE NAME

USERNAME

PASSWORD

EMAIL

NOTE

WEBSITE NAME

USERNAME

PASSWORD

EMAIL

NOTE

WEBSITE NAME

USERNAME

PASSWORD

EMAIL

NOTE

WEBSITE NAME

USERNAME

PASSWORD

EMAIL

NOTE

WEBSITE NAME

USERNAME

PASSWORD

EMAIL

NOTE

WEBSITE NAME

USERNAME

PASSWORD

EMAIL

NOTE

WEBSITE NAME

USERNAME

PASSWORD

EMAIL

NOTE

WEBSITE NAME

USERNAME

PASSWORD

EMAIL

NOTE

WEBSITE NAME

USERNAME

PASSWORD

EMAIL

NOTE

WEBSITE NAME

USERNAME

PASSWORD

EMAIL

NOTE

WEBSITE NAME

USERNAME

PASSWORD

EMAIL

NOTE

WEBSITE NAME

USERNAME

PASSWORD

EMAIL

NOTE

WEBSITE NAME

USERNAME

PASSWORD

EMAIL

NOTE

WEBSITE NAME

USERNAME

PASSWORD

EMAIL

NOTE

WEBSITE NAME

USERNAME

PASSWORD

EMAIL

NOTE

WEBSITE NAME

USERNAME

PASSWORD

EMAIL

NOTE

WEBSITE NAME

USERNAME

PASSWORD

EMAIL

NOTE

WEBSITE NAME

USERNAME

PASSWORD

EMAIL

NOTE

WEBSITE NAME

USERNAME

PASSWORD

EMAIL

NOTE

WEBSITE NAME

USERNAME

PASSWORD

EMAIL

NOTE

WEBSITE NAME

USERNAME

PASSWORD

EMAIL

NOTE

WEBSITE NAME

USERNAME

PASSWORD

EMAIL

NOTE

WEBSITE NAME

USERNAME

PASSWORD

EMAIL

NOTE

WEBSITE NAME

USERNAME

PASSWORD

EMAIL

NOTE

WEBSITE NAME

USERNAME

PASSWORD

EMAIL

NOTE

WEBSITE NAME

USERNAME

PASSWORD

EMAIL

NOTE

WEBSITE NAME

USERNAME

PASSWORD

EMAIL

NOTE

WEBSITE NAME

USERNAME

PASSWORD

EMAIL

NOTE

WEBSITE NAME

USERNAME

PASSWORD

EMAIL

NOTE

WEBSITE NAME

USERNAME

PASSWORD

EMAIL

NOTE

WEBSITE NAME

USERNAME

PASSWORD

EMAIL

NOTE

WEBSITE NAME

USERNAME

PASSWORD

EMAIL

NOTE

WEBSITE NAME

USERNAME

PASSWORD

EMAIL

NOTE

WEBSITE NAME

USERNAME

PASSWORD

EMAIL

NOTE

WEBSITE NAME

USERNAME

PASSWORD

EMAIL

NOTE

WEBSITE NAME

USERNAME

PASSWORD

EMAIL

NOTE

WEBSITE NAME

USERNAME

PASSWORD

EMAIL

NOTE

WEBSITE NAME

USERNAME

PASSWORD

EMAIL

NOTE

WEBSITE NAME

USERNAME

PASSWORD

EMAIL

NOTE

WEBSITE NAME

USERNAME

PASSWORD

EMAIL

NOTE

WEBSITE NAME

USERNAME

PASSWORD

EMAIL

NOTE

WEBSITE NAME

USERNAME

PASSWORD

EMAIL

NOTE

WEBSITE NAME

USERNAME

PASSWORD

EMAIL

NOTE

WEBSITE NAME

USERNAME

PASSWORD

EMAIL

NOTE

WEBSITE NAME

USERNAME

PASSWORD

EMAIL

NOTE

WEBSITE NAME

USERNAME

PASSWORD

EMAIL

NOTE

WEBSITE NAME

USERNAME

PASSWORD

EMAIL

NOTE

WEBSITE NAME

USERNAME

PASSWORD

EMAIL

NOTE

WEBSITE NAME

USERNAME

PASSWORD

EMAIL

NOTE

WEBSITE NAME

USERNAME

PASSWORD

EMAIL

NOTE

WEBSITE NAME

USERNAME

PASSWORD

EMAIL

NOTE

WEBSITE NAME

USERNAME

PASSWORD

EMAIL

NOTE

WEBSITE NAME

USERNAME

PASSWORD

EMAIL

NOTE

WEBSITE NAME

USERNAME

PASSWORD

EMAIL

NOTE

WEBSITE NAME

USERNAME

PASSWORD

EMAIL

NOTE

WEBSITE NAME

USERNAME

PASSWORD

EMAIL

NOTE

WEBSITE NAME

USERNAME

PASSWORD

EMAIL

NOTE

WEBSITE NAME

USERNAME

PASSWORD

EMAIL

NOTE

WEBSITE NAME

USERNAME

PASSWORD

EMAIL

NOTE

WEBSITE NAME

USERNAME

PASSWORD

EMAIL

NOTE

WEBSITE NAME

USERNAME

PASSWORD

EMAIL

NOTE

WEBSITE NAME

USERNAME

PASSWORD

EMAIL

NOTE

WEBSITE NAME

USERNAME

PASSWORD

EMAIL

NOTE

WEBSITE NAME

USERNAME

PASSWORD

EMAIL

NOTE

WEBSITE NAME

USERNAME

PASSWORD

EMAIL

NOTE

WEBSITE NAME

USERNAME

PASSWORD

EMAIL

NOTE

WEBSITE NAME

USERNAME

PASSWORD

EMAIL

NOTE

WEBSITE NAME

USERNAME

PASSWORD

EMAIL

NOTE

WEBSITE NAME

USERNAME

PASSWORD

EMAIL

NOTE

WEBSITE NAME

USERNAME

PASSWORD

EMAIL

NOTE

WEBSITE NAME

USERNAME

PASSWORD

EMAIL

NOtE

WEBSITE NAME

USERNAME

PASSWORD

EMAIL

NOtE

WEBSITE NAME

USERNAME

PASSWORD

EMAIL

NOtE

WEBSITE NAME

USERNAME

PASSWORD

EMAIL

NOtE

WEBSITE NAME

USERNAME

PASSWORD

EMAIL

NOTE

WEBSITE NAME

USERNAME

PASSWORD

EMAIL

NOTE

WEBSITE NAME

USERNAME

PASSWORD

EMAIL

NOTE

WEBSITE NAME

USERNAME

PASSWORD

EMAIL

NOTE

WEBSITE NAME

USERNAME

PASSWORD

EMAIL

NOTE

WEBSITE NAME

USERNAME

PASSWORD

EMAIL

NOTE

WEBSITE NAME

USERNAME

PASSWORD

EMAIL

NOTE

WEBSITE NAME

USERNAME

PASSWORD

EMAIL

NOTE

WEBSITE NAME

USERNAME

PASSWORD

EMAIL

NOTE

WEBSITE NAME

USERNAME

PASSWORD

EMAIL

NOTE

WEBSITE NAME

USERNAME

PASSWORD

EMAIL

NOTE

WEBSITE NAME

USERNAME

PASSWORD

EMAIL

NOTE

WEBSITE NAME

USERNAME

PASSWORD

EMAIL

NOTE

WEBSITE NAME

USERNAME

PASSWORD

EMAIL

NOTE

WEBSITE NAME

USERNAME

PASSWORD

EMAIL

NOTE

WEBSITE NAME

USERNAME

PASSWORD

EMAIL

NOTE

WEBSITE NAME

USERNAME

PASSWORD

EMAIL

NOTE

WEBSITE NAME

USERNAME

PASSWORD

EMAIL

NOTE

WEBSITE NAME

USERNAME

PASSWORD

EMAIL

NOTE

WEBSITE NAME

USERNAME

PASSWORD

EMAIL

NOTE

WEBSITE NAME

USERNAME

PASSWORD

EMAIL

NOTE

WEBSITE NAME

USERNAME

PASSWORD

EMAIL

NOTE

WEBSITE NAME

USERNAME

PASSWORD

EMAIL

NOTE

WEBSITE NAME

USERNAME

PASSWORD

EMAIL

NOTE

WEBSITE NAME

USERNAME

PASSWORD

EMAIL

NOTE

WEBSITE NAME

USERNAME

PASSWORD

EMAIL

NOTE

WEBSITE NAME

USERNAME

PASSWORD

EMAIL

NOTE

WEBSITE NAME

USERNAME

PASSWORD

EMAIL

NOTE

WEBSITE NAME

USERNAME

PASSWORD

EMAIL

NOTE

WEBSITE NAME

USERNAME

PASSWORD

EMAIL

NOTE

WEBSITE NAME

USERNAME

PASSWORD

EMAIL

NOTE

WEBSITE NAME

USERNAME

PASSWORD

EMAIL

NOTE

WEBSITE NAME

USERNAME

PASSWORD

EMAIL

NOTE

WEBSITE NAME

USERNAME

PASSWORD

EMAIL

NOTE

WEBSITE NAME

USERNAME

PASSWORD

EMAIL

NOTE

WEBSITE NAME

USERNAME

PASSWORD

EMAIL

NOTE

WEBSITE NAME

USERNAME

PASSWORD

EMAIL

NOTE

WEBSITE NAME

USERNAME

PASSWORD

EMAIL

NOTE

WEBSITE NAME

USERNAME

PASSWORD

EMAIL

NOTE

WEBSITE NAME

USERNAME

PASSWORD

EMAIL

NOTE

WEBSITE NAME

USERNAME

PASSWORD

EMAIL

NOTE

WEBSITE NAME

USERNAME

PASSWORD

EMAIL

NOTE

WEBSITE NAME

USERNAME

PASSWORD

EMAIL

NOTE

WEBSITE NAME

USERNAME

PASSWORD

EMAIL

NOTE

WEBSITE NAME

USERNAME

PASSWORD

EMAIL

NOTE

WEBSITE NAME

USERNAME

PASSWORD

EMAIL

NOTE

WEBSITE NAME

USERNAME

PASSWORD

EMAIL

NOTE

WEBSITE NAME

USERNAME

PASSWORD

EMAIL

NOTE

WEBSITE NAME

USERNAME

PASSWORD

EMAIL

NOTE

WEBSITE NAME

USERNAME

PASSWORD

EMAIL

NOTE

WEBSITE NAME

USERNAME

PASSWORD

EMAIL

NOTE

WEBSITE NAME

USERNAME

PASSWORD

EMAIL

NOTE

WEBSITE NAME

USERNAME

PASSWORD

EMAIL

NOTE

WEBSITE NAME

USERNAME

PASSWORD

EMAIL

NOTE

WEBSITE NAME

USERNAME

PASSWORD

EMAIL

NOTE

WEBSITE NAME

USERNAME

PASSWORD

EMAIL

NOTE

WEBSITE NAME

USERNAME

PASSWORD

EMAIL

NOTE

WEBSITE NAME

USERNAME

PASSWORD

EMAIL

NOTE

WEBSITE NAME

USERNAME

PASSWORD

EMAIL

NOTE

WEBSITE NAME

USERNAME

PASSWORD

EMAIL

NOTE

WEBSITE NAME

USERNAME

PASSWORD

EMAIL

NOTE

WEBSITE NAME

USERNAME

PASSWORD

EMAIL

NOTE

WEBSITE NAME

USERNAME

PASSWORD

EMAIL

NOTE

WEBSITE NAME

USERNAME

PASSWORD

EMAIL

NOTE

WEBSITE NAME

USERNAME

PASSWORD

EMAIL

NOTE

WEBSITE NAME

USERNAME

PASSWORD

EMAIL

NOTE

WEBSITE NAME

USERNAME

PASSWORD

EMAIL

NOTE

WEBSITE NAME

USERNAME

PASSWORD

EMAIL

NOTE

WEBSITE NAME

USERNAME

PASSWORD

EMAIL

NOTE

WEBSITE NAME

USERNAME

PASSWORD

EMAIL

NOTE

WEBSITE NAME

USERNAME

PASSWORD

EMAIL

NOTE

WEBSITE NAME

USERNAME

PASSWORD

EMAIL

NOTE

WEBSITE NAME

USERNAME

PASSWORD

EMAIL

NOTE

WEBSITE NAME

USERNAME

PASSWORD

EMAIL

NOTE

WEBSITE NAME

USERNAME

PASSWORD

EMAIL

NOTE

WEBSITE NAME

USERNAME

PASSWORD

EMAIL

NOTE

WEBSITE NAME

USERNAME

PASSWORD

EMAIL

NOTE

WEBSITE NAME

USERNAME

PASSWORD

EMAIL

NOTE

WEBSITE NAME

USERNAME

PASSWORD

EMAIL

NOTE

WEBSITE NAME

USERNAME

PASSWORD

EMAIL

NOTE

WEBSITE NAME

USERNAME

PASSWORD

EMAIL

NOTE

WEBSITE NAME

USERNAME

PASSWORD

EMAIL

NOTE

WEBSITE NAME

USERNAME

PASSWORD

EMAIL

NOTE

WEBSITE NAME

USERNAME

PASSWORD

EMAIL

NOTE

WEBSITE NAME

USERNAME

PASSWORD

EMAIL

NOTE

WEBSITE NAME

USERNAME

PASSWORD

EMAIL

NOTE

WEBSITE NAME

USERNAME

PASSWORD

EMAIL

NOTE

WEBSITE NAME

USERNAME

PASSWORD

EMAIL

NOTE

WEBSITE NAME

USERNAME

PASSWORD

EMAIL

NOTE

WEBSITE NAME

USERNAME

PASSWORD

EMAIL

NOTE

WEBSITE NAME

USERNAME

PASSWORD

EMAIL

NOTE

WEBSITE NAME

USERNAME

PASSWORD

EMAIL

NOTE

WEBSITE NAME

USERNAME

PASSWORD

EMAIL

NOTE

WEBSITE NAME

USERNAME

PASSWORD

EMAIL

NOTE

WEBSITE NAME

USERNAME

PASSWORD

EMAIL

NOTE

WEBSITE NAME

USERNAME

PASSWORD

EMAIL

NOTE

WEBSITE NAME

USERNAME

PASSWORD

EMAIL

NOTE

WEBSITE NAME

USERNAME

PASSWORD

EMAIL

NOTE

WEBSITE NAME

USERNAME

PASSWORD

EMAIL

NOTE

WEBSITE NAME

USERNAME

PASSWORD

EMAIL

NOTE

WEBSITE NAME

USERNAME

PASSWORD

EMAIL

NOTE

WEBSITE NAME

USERNAME

PASSWORD

EMAIL

NOTE

WEBSITE NAME

USERNAME

PASSWORD

EMAIL

NOTE

WEBSITE NAME

USERNAME

PASSWORD

EMAIL

NOTE

WEBSITE NAME

USERNAME

PASSWORD

EMAIL

NOTE

WEBSITE NAME

USERNAME

PASSWORD

EMAIL

NOTE

WEBSITE NAME

USERNAME

PASSWORD

EMAIL

NOTE

WEBSITE NAME

USERNAME

PASSWORD

EMAIL

NOTE

WEBSITE NAME

USERNAME

PASSWORD

EMAIL

NOTE

WEBSITE NAME

USERNAME

PASSWORD

EMAIL

NOTE

WEBSITE NAME

USERNAME

PASSWORD

EMAIL

NOTE

WEBSITE NAME

USERNAME

PASSWORD

EMAIL

NOTE

WEBSITE NAME

USERNAME

PASSWORD

EMAIL

NOTE

WEBSITE NAME

USERNAME

PASSWORD

EMAIL

NOTE

WEBSITE NAME

USERNAME

PASSWORD

EMAIL

NOTE

WEBSITE NAME

USERNAME

PASSWORD

EMAIL

NOTE

WEBSITE NAME

USERNAME

PASSWORD

EMAIL

NOTE

WEBSITE NAME

USERNAME

PASSWORD

EMAIL

NOTE

WEBSITE NAME

USERNAME

PASSWORD

EMAIL

NOTE

WEBSITE NAME

USERNAME

PASSWORD

EMAIL

NOTE

WEBSITE NAME

USERNAME

PASSWORD

EMAIL

NOTE

WEBSITE NAME

USERNAME

PASSWORD

EMAIL

NOTE

WEBSITE NAME

USERNAME

PASSWORD

EMAIL

NOTE

WEBSITE NAME

USERNAME

PASSWORD

EMAIL

NOTE

WEBSITE NAME

USERNAME

PASSWORD

EMAIL

NOTE

WEBSITE NAME

USERNAME

PASSWORD

EMAIL

NOTE

WEBSITE NAME

USERNAME

PASSWORD

EMAIL

NOTE

WEBSITE NAME

USERNAME

PASSWORD

EMAIL

NOTE

WEBSITE NAME

USERNAME

PASSWORD

EMAIL

NOTE

WEBSITE NAME

USERNAME

PASSWORD

EMAIL

NOTE

WEBSITE NAME

USERNAME

PASSWORD

EMAIL

NOTE

WEBSITE NAME

USERNAME

PASSWORD

EMAIL

NOTE

WEBSITE NAME

USERNAME

PASSWORD

EMAIL

NOTE

WEBSITE NAME

USERNAME

PASSWORD

EMAIL

NOTE

WEBSITE NAME

USERNAME

PASSWORD

EMAIL

NOTE

WEBSITE NAME

USERNAME

PASSWORD

EMAIL

NOTE

WEBSITE NAME

USERNAME

PASSWORD

EMAIL

NOTE

WEBSITE NAME

USERNAME

PASSWORD

EMAIL

NOTE

WEBSITE NAME

USERNAME

PASSWORD

EMAIL

NOTE

WEBSITE NAME

USERNAME

PASSWORD

EMAIL

NOTE

WEBSITE NAME

USERNAME

PASSWORD

EMAIL

NOTE

WEBSITE NAME

USERNAME

PASSWORD

EMAIL

NOTE

WEBSITE NAME

USERNAME

PASSWORD

EMAIL

NOTE

WEBSITE NAME

USERNAME

PASSWORD

EMAIL

NOTE

WEBSITE NAME

USERNAME

PASSWORD

EMAIL

NOTE

WEBSITE NAME

USERNAME

PASSWORD

EMAIL

NOTE

WEBSITE NAME

USERNAME

PASSWORD

EMAIL

NOTE

WEBSITE NAME

USERNAME

PASSWORD

EMAIL

NOTE

WEBSITE NAME

USERNAME

PASSWORD

EMAIL

NOTE

WEBSITE NAME

USERNAME

PASSWORD

EMAIL

NOTE

WEBSITE NAME

USERNAME

PASSWORD

EMAIL

NOTE

WEBSITE NAME

USERNAME

PASSWORD

EMAIL

NOTE

WEBSITE NAME

USERNAME

PASSWORD

EMAIL

NOTE

WEBSITE NAME

USERNAME

PASSWORD

EMAIL

NOTE

WEBSITE NAME

USERNAME

PASSWORD

EMAIL

NOTE

WEBSITE NAME

USERNAME

PASSWORD

EMAIL

NOTE

WEBSITE NAME

USERNAME

PASSWORD

EMAIL

NOTE

WEBSITE NAME

USERNAME

PASSWORD

EMAIL

NOTE

WEBSITE NAME

USERNAME

PASSWORD

EMAIL

NOTE

WEBSITE NAME

USERNAME

PASSWORD

EMAIL

NOTE

WEBSITE NAME

USERNAME

PASSWORD

EMAIL

NOTE

WEBSITE NAME

USERNAME

PASSWORD

EMAIL

NOTE

WEBSITE NAME

USERNAME

PASSWORD

EMAIL

NOTE

WEBSITE NAME

USERNAME

PASSWORD

EMAIL

NOTE

WEBSITE NAME

USERNAME

PASSWORD

EMAIL

NOTE

WEBSITE NAME

USERNAME

PASSWORD

EMAIL

NOTE

WEBSITE NAME

USERNAME

PASSWORD

EMAIL

NOTE

WEBSITE NAME

USERNAME

PASSWORD

EMAIL

NOTE

WEBSITE NAME

USERNAME

PASSWORD

EMAIL

NOTE

WEBSITE NAME

USERNAME

PASSWORD

EMAIL

NOTE

WEBSITE NAME

USERNAME

PASSWORD

EMAIL

NOTE

WEBSITE NAME

USERNAME

PASSWORD

EMAIL

NOTE

WEBSITE NAME

USERNAME

PASSWORD

EMAIL

NOTE

WEBSITE NAME

USERNAME

PASSWORD

EMAIL

NOTE

WEBSITE NAME

USERNAME

PASSWORD

EMAIL

NOTE

WEBSITE NAME

USERNAME

PASSWORD

EMAIL

NOTE

WEBSITE NAME

USERNAME

PASSWORD

EMAIL

NOTE

WEBSITE NAME

USERNAME

PASSWORD

EMAIL

NOTE

WEBSITE NAME

USERNAME

PASSWORD

EMAIL

NOTE

WEBSITE NAME

USERNAME

PASSWORD

EMAIL

NOTE

WEBSITE NAME

USERNAME

PASSWORD

EMAIL

NOTE

WEBSITE NAME

USERNAME

PASSWORD

EMAIL

NOTE

WEBSITE NAME

USERNAME

PASSWORD

EMAIL

NOTE

WEBSITE NAME

USERNAME

PASSWORD

EMAIL

NOTE

WEBSITE NAME

USERNAME

PASSWORD

EMAIL

NOTE

WEBSITE NAME

USERNAME

PASSWORD

EMAIL

NOTE

WEBSITE NAME

USERNAME

PASSWORD

EMAIL

NOTE

WEBSITE NAME

USERNAME

PASSWORD

EMAIL

NOTE

WEBSITE NAME

USERNAME

PASSWORD

EMAIL

NOTE

WEBSITE NAME

USERNAME

PASSWORD

EMAIL

NOTE

WEBSITE NAME

USERNAME

PASSWORD

EMAIL

NOTE

WEBSITE NAME

USERNAME

PASSWORD

EMAIL

NOTE

WEBSITE NAME

USERNAME

PASSWORD

EMAIL

NOTE

WEBSITE NAME

USERNAME

PASSWORD

EMAIL

NOTE

WEBSITE NAME

USERNAME

PASSWORD

EMAIL

NOTE

WEBSITE NAME

USERNAME

PASSWORD

EMAIL

NOTE

WEBSITE NAME

USERNAME

PASSWORD

EMAIL

NOTE

WEBSITE NAME

USERNAME

PASSWORD

EMAIL

NOTE

WEBSITE NAME

USERNAME

PASSWORD

EMAIL

NOTE

WEBSITE NAME

USERNAME

PASSWORD

EMAIL

NOTE

WEBSITE NAME

USERNAME

PASSWORD

EMAIL

NOTE

WEBSITE NAME

USERNAME

PASSWORD

EMAIL

NOTE

WEBSITE NAME

USERNAME

PASSWORD

EMAIL

NOTE

WEBSITE NAME

USERNAME

PASSWORD

EMAIL

NOTE

WEBSITE NAME

USERNAME

PASSWORD

EMAIL

NOTE

WEBSITE NAME

USERNAME

PASSWORD

EMAIL

NOTE

WEBSITE NAME

USERNAME

PASSWORD

EMAIL

NOTE

WEBSITE NAME

USERNAME

PASSWORD

EMAIL

NOTE

WEBSITE NAME

USERNAME

PASSWORD

EMAIL

NOTE

WEBSITE NAME

USERNAME

PASSWORD

EMAIL

NOTE

WEBSITE NAME

USERNAME

PASSWORD

EMAIL

NOTE

WEBSITE NAME

USERNAME

PASSWORD

EMAIL

NOTE

WEBSITE NAME

USERNAME

PASSWORD

EMAIL

NOTE

WEBSITE NAME

USERNAME

PASSWORD

EMAIL

NOTE

WEBSITE NAME

USERNAME

PASSWORD

EMAIL

NOTE

WEBSITE NAME

USERNAME

PASSWORD

EMAIL

NOTE

WEBSITE NAME

USERNAME

PASSWORD

EMAIL

NOTE

WEBSITE NAME

USERNAME

PASSWORD

EMAIL

NOTE

WEBSITE NAME

USERNAME

PASSWORD

EMAIL

NOTE

WEBSITE NAME

USERNAME

PASSWORD

EMAIL

NOTE

WEBSITE NAME

USERNAME

PASSWORD

EMAIL

NOTE

WEBSITE NAME

USERNAME

PASSWORD

EMAIL

NOTE

WEBSITE NAME

USERNAME

PASSWORD

EMAIL

NOTE

WEBSITE NAME

USERNAME

PASSWORD

EMAIL

NOTE

WEBSITE NAME

USERNAME

PASSWORD

EMAIL

NOTE

WEBSITE NAME

USERNAME

PASSWORD

EMAIL

NOTE

WEBSITE NAME

USERNAME

PASSWORD

EMAIL

NOTE

WEBSITE NAME

USERNAME

PASSWORD

EMAIL

NOTE

WEBSITE NAME

USERNAME

PASSWORD

EMAIL

NOTE

WEBSITE NAME

USERNAME

PASSWORD

EMAIL

NOTE

WEBSITE NAME

USERNAME

PASSWORD

EMAIL

NOTE

WEBSITE NAME

USERNAME

PASSWORD

EMAIL

NOTE

WEBSITE NAME

USERNAME

PASSWORD

EMAIL

NOTE

WEBSITE NAME

USERNAME

PASSWORD

EMAIL

NOTE

WEBSITE NAME

USERNAME

PASSWORD

EMAIL

NOTE

WEBSITE NAME

USERNAME

PASSWORD

EMAIL

NOTE

WEBSITE NAME

USERNAME

PASSWORD

EMAIL

NOTE

WEBSITE NAME

USERNAME

PASSWORD

EMAIL

NOTE

WEBSITE NAME

USERNAME

PASSWORD

EMAIL

NOTE

WEBSITE NAME

USERNAME

PASSWORD

EMAIL

NOTE

WEBSITE NAME

USERNAME

PASSWORD

EMAIL

NOTE

WEBSITE NAME

USERNAME

PASSWORD

EMAIL

NOTE

WEBSITE NAME

USERNAME

PASSWORD

EMAIL

NOTE

WEBSITE NAME

USERNAME

PASSWORD

EMAIL

NOTE

WEBSITE NAME

USERNAME

PASSWORD

EMAIL

NOTE

WEBSITE NAME

USERNAME

PASSWORD

EMAIL

NOTE

WEBSITE NAME

USERNAME

PASSWORD

EMAIL

NOTE

WEBSITE NAME

USERNAME

PASSWORD

EMAIL

NOTE

WEBSITE NAME

USERNAME

PASSWORD

EMAIL

NOTE

WEBSITE NAME

USERNAME

PASSWORD

EMAIL

NOTE

WEBSITE NAME

USERNAME

PASSWORD

EMAIL

NOTE

WEBSITE NAME

USERNAME

PASSWORD

EMAIL

NOTE

WEBSITE NAME

USERNAME

PASSWORD

EMAIL

NOTE

WEBSITE NAME

USERNAME

PASSWORD

EMAIL

NOTE

WEBSITE NAME

USERNAME

PASSWORD

EMAIL

NOTE

WEBSITE NAME

USERNAME

PASSWORD

EMAIL

NOTE

WEBSITE NAME

USERNAME

PASSWORD

EMAIL

NOTE

WEBSITE NAME

USERNAME

PASSWORD

EMAIL

NOTE

WEBSITE NAME

USERNAME

PASSWORD

EMAIL

NOTE

WEBSITE NAME

USERNAME

PASSWORD

EMAIL

NOTE

WEBSITE NAME

USERNAME

PASSWORD

EMAIL

NOTE

WEBSITE NAME

USERNAME

PASSWORD

EMAIL

NOTE

WEBSITE NAME

USERNAME

PASSWORD

EMAIL

NOTE

WEBSITE NAME

USERNAME

PASSWORD

EMAIL

NOTE